Mommy Needs a Minute

Claire E. Parsons

Illustrated by

Naomi L. Hudson

scarlet oak press

scarletoakpress.com

scarlet oak press.

For permissions and information about special discounts for bulk purchases, contact Scarlet Oak Press at contact@scarletoakpress.com.

ISBN: 978-1-954974-17-3 (eBook)

ISBN: 978-1-954974-16-6 (Hard Cover)

Library of Congress Control Number: 2023902957

Published by Scarlet Oak Press (scarletoakpress.com)

Dedication

To our darling babies.

C.E.P. & N.L.H.

Mommy Needs a Minute

Claire E. Parsons

Illustrated by

Naomi L. Hudson

I love you so, my darling *babies*,

that it makes my heart ache…

But I have to tell you, *Sweeties*,

that Mommy needs a break.

It's been a day, an awful day.

Do you know what I mean?

A day where nothing goes your way,

and there is no routine.

I'm feeling a bit tired,

and stressed out to the Max !

I don't want to get wired.

Can you let me Relax ?

I need to let my mind unwind…

To stop and just to sit.

So if you could, oh *pretty* please,

Give me one tiny minute.

Maybe five would be better still,

so I could sit and breathe.

Or hey, if you could manage it,

ten might give such relief.

You know what I wish you would say? That twenty would be fine!

Holy moly, that would be just great!

It would make me feel *Sublime*.

I know you think it all so strange

That I enjoy doing nothing.

But when you get to my old age,

just breathing can be quite something.

I don't have just myself to think of

I always think of you.

And piling up on top of that

is a list of things to do.

I'm busy and important, you see.

Many people depend on me.

My calendar is almost always full,

and life is never, ever dull.

So it helps me every now and then literally

to just **STOP**.

To sit and find  a little zen.

And let everything drop.

It gives me a little bit of time

To be -- just be -- with me.

To be myself and see myself.

It helps me to feel free.

Go hang with Dad or play with toys
or read an awesome book.

After some time, I will come back

to play with and care for you.

Because rest will bring my fun back,

and I hope, my energy, too.

So thank you, my dear little ones,

for giving me some peace.

I know it's not natural to you,

though it makes me

feel at ease.

I love you, my darling *babies*.

I want to give you my best.

For me, it means that sometimes
Mommy needs a minute to rest.

About the Author

Claire E. Parsons is a litigation and employment lawyer in Cincinnati, Ohio. She's also a certified mindfulness and compassion teacher, the founder of the Brilliant Legal Mind blog, and the author of the book

How to be a Badass Lawyer: The Simple and Unexpected Guide to Less Stress and Greater Personal Development Through Mindfulness and Compassion. She regularly presents and teaches about mindfulness and compassion to fellow lawyers and professionals.

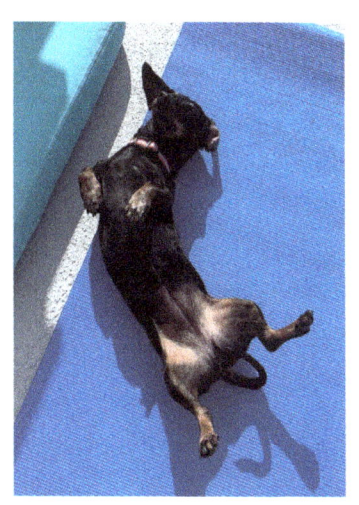

Claire lives in Northern Kentucky with her husband, Brian, daughters, Sophie and Elinor, and miniature dachshund, Lyra. Claire regularly makes up silly rhymes and songs for her girls.

She and Naomi became friends after their daughters met at daycare. Claire is glad that Naomi's passion for drawing brought her silly rhymes to life in this book.

About the Illustrator

Naomi L. Hudson loves both the arts and sciences. By day she is a health science researcher, and by night she is crafty and loves to explore with her family. In any given week, it is not unusual for Naomi to draw pictures for her daughters' lunchboxes, paint an aquarium to look like a mermaid's treasure trove, or bake fantastical cakes or cookies to celebrate a birthday, life event, or a Tuesday.

Naomi studied biology at Berea College, which sits in a community known as a haven for arts in Kentucky. She then obtained degrees in environmental health and epidemiology before starting her work as a researcher. She continued crafting, creating art, and baking as a way to connect with friends and family. Naomi is also the illustrator for *Kennedi Comes Home* by Sharron and Kennedi Sanders, which was published in 2022.

Naomi lives with her husband, Josh, and two daughters, Lydia and Kayleigh, along with their two dogs.

.

www.ingramcontent.com/pod-product-compliance
Lightning Source LLC
Chambersburg PA
CBHW051603120626
46551CB00013B/1647